Awesome Fac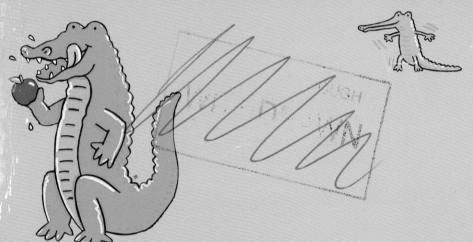
about
Crocodiles

D1325183

0040747689

se

A n
due
show
inter
dan
www

This edition printed in 2000
© Aladdin Books Ltd 1998
Produced by
Aladdin Books Ltd
28 Percy Street
London W1P 0LD

ISBN 0-7496-3935-0 (paperback)

Previously published in hardcover
in the series "I Didn't Know That"
ISBN 0-7496-3244-5 (hardback)

First published in Great Britain in 1998 by
Aladdin Books/Watts Books
96 Leonard Street
London EC2A 4XD

Editor: Liz White
Design: David West Children's Books
Designer: Robert Perry
Illustrators: James Field – Simon Girling Associates,
Jo Moore

Printed in the U.A.E.

All rights reserved
A CIP catalogue record for this book is available from
the British Library

Awesome Facts
about
Crocodiles

Kate Petty

597.98

0040747689
12/00

A l a d d i n / W a t t s
L o n d o n • S y d n e y

Contents

Introduction

Did *you* know that reptiles never stop growing? ... that some crocodiles eat people? ... that others are bred on farms, just like sheep and cows?

Discover for yourself amazing facts about crocodiles and alligators – the differences between them, where they live, what they eat, how they have babies and more.

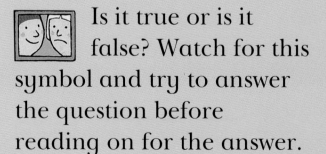

Look out for this symbol which means there is a fun project for you to try.

Is it true or is it false? Watch for this symbol and try to answer the question before reading on for the answer.

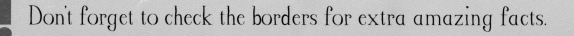

Don't forget to check the borders for extra amazing facts.

What is a crocodile?

Crocodiles are *reptiles* that have been around since the dinosaur age. A crocodile looked much the same then as it does today. However crocodiles unlike dinosaurs weren't wiped out 65 million years ago.

SEARCH & FIND Can you find the big dinosaur? **FIND & SEARCH**

Sarcosuchus

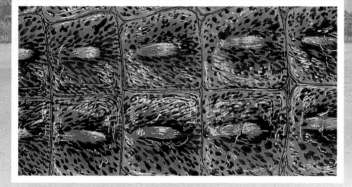

A crocodile's armour-plated skin is made up of horny scales called scutes, with extra protection from the bony plates just below the surface.

Crocodiles belong to the *crocodilian* family. So do their American cousins, the alligators (there is also a rare Chinese alligator) and so do caimans and the gharial.

Crocodile

Gharial

Alligator

Caiman

Some *prehistoric* crocodiles were giants up to 16m long. They would almost certainly have preyed on other reptiles, including small dinosaurs.

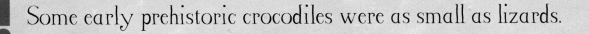

Some early prehistoric crocodiles were as small as lizards.

! Egyptians in the town Crokodilopolis, had a crocodile god.

True or false?
Crocodiles and alligators never meet.

Answer: **False**
The American crocodile is rare and the American alligator is flourishing, but both are found in the swamps of Florida.

Saltwater crocodile

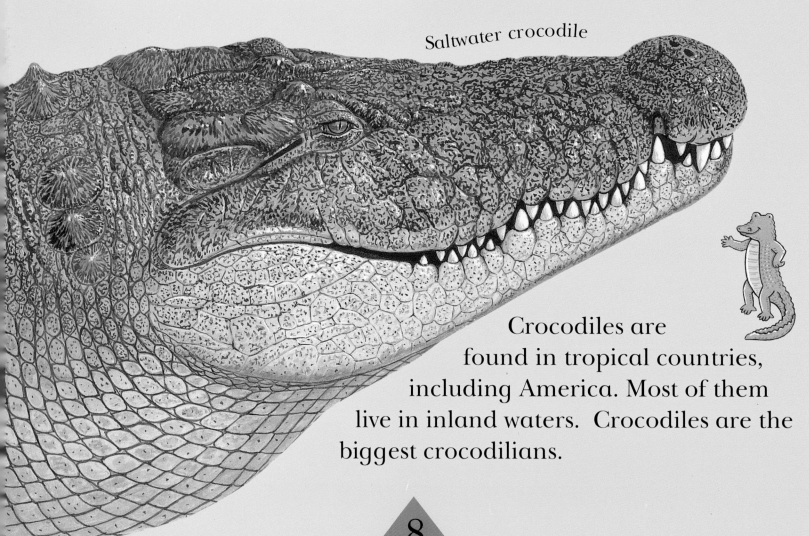

Crocodiles are found in tropical countries, including America. Most of them live in inland waters. Crocodiles are the biggest crocodilians.

8

Most alligators (apart from the Chinese one) are found in the Americas. They have squarer jaws than crocodiles.

American alligator

Our baby teeth are replaced once by grown-up teeth but a crocodile's teeth can be replaced 40 times as they wear down.

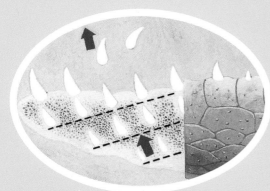

Crocodile or alligator?

You can tell the difference between a crocodile and an alligator by its teeth. When an alligator's jaw is closed you can only see the top teeth. A crocodile shows some of its lower teeth too.

The name 'alligator' comes from 'el lagarto', Spanish for 'lizard'.

A little bird, the Egyptian plover, is safe within the jaws of a Nile crocodile. It picks out *parasites* and leeches, doing the crocodile a favour.

Nile crocodile

Reptiles

Reptiles are *cold-blooded.* Crocodiles bask in the sun for warmth and cool off in the water. They yawn to keep cool as the cool air on the thinner skin on the inside of their mouths stops them from overheating.

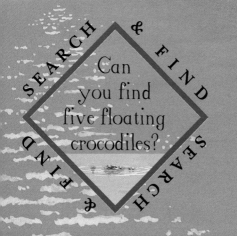

SEARCH & FIND SEARCH & FIND ⋆ Can you find five floating crocodiles?

Reptiles never stop growing throughout their lives. Young crocodiles grow 30cm a year. Imagine if that happened to you!

The saltwater crocodile from south-east Asia is a giant, the biggest of all living reptiles. The record is held by an individual that measured 8.6m and weighed two tonnes. The smallest crocodile is the rare African dwarf which measures only 1.5m.

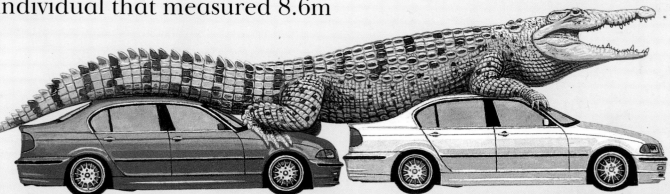

In the film *Peter Pan* a crocodile swallowed a clock.

Life in the water

Crocodiles spend many hours in the water. They lie submerged and completely still, pretending to be floating logs. Their eyes and nostrils are on top of their heads so they can see and breathe as they lie in wait for their prey.

SEARCH & FIND & SEARCH & FIND
Can you find the baby caiman?

Some crocodiles stay under water for an hour. Special flaps close off their nostrils, throats and ears. A special, clear eyelid protects the eyes.

Black caiman

A crocodile's back feet are webbed, like a frog's. Webbed feet help it to steer and manoeuvre quickly in the water if it needs to.

Fish-eating crocodiles, like the Australian *freshwater* crocodile (right), often have long, thin snouts, good for catching fish, and a streamlined body.

❗ Caimans are preyed on by anaconda snakes.

Catching prey

Crocodiles and alligators move fast, running and swimming, to launch a surprise attack on their prey. Alligators can even leap into the air from the water if their lunch is high up. Smaller crocodiles will climb trees to catch insects and snails.

American alligator

The gharial catches several fish at once with a sideways swipe of its head and grips them in its sharp teeth.

True or false?

Some crocodiles are muggers.

Answer: **True**

One type of Indian crocodile is called a mugger. It is a man-eater and its main victims are women washing clothes and children playing on the riverbank.

15

Feeding

When catching a large animal, a crocodile lunges and knocks its prey into the water. It will eat a large animal all at once and *digest* it over a long period of time. Some crocodiles only eat twice a year.

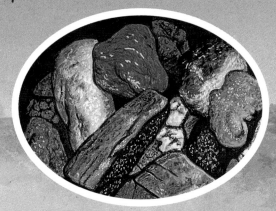

Stones have been found in the stomachs of crocodiles. They swallow them to help grind up their food.

A crocodile's teeth are designed for gripping, not for chewing. It tears the meat off in chunks and swallows them whole.

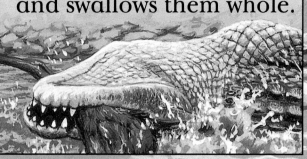

Crocodiles have very strong jaws that lock on to their prey.

Nile crocodiles help each other when they feed. One holds the prey down while the other feeds off it. Groups of young Nile crocodiles cooperate to catch fish.

Wildebeest

The gharial's name comes from a word for 'pot' and describes the shape of the lump on the male's nose (left). The 'pot' works as an amplifier for his mating call.

Nile crocodile

In the mating season male crocodiles behave strangely! They fight to decide who is strongest. The American crocodile (below) snaps and splashes the water with his jaws to keep others out of his *territory*.

Crocodiles can communicate using smell.

Courting couples put on *displays*, rubbing heads or lying alongside each other with their mouths open. This female saltwater crocodile raises her head out of the water to show that she wants to mate.

Mating

A male Nile crocodile growls and lashes its tail as a threat to other males in the mating season. It will sometimes lower its head into the water and blow bubbles through its nostrils to attract a mate.

19

When a baby crocodile hatches it has a sharp point on its snout called an egg tooth. It needs this to break its way out of the hard-shelled egg where it has lain tightly curled.

Crocodile parents guard the nest against raiders such as birds or baboons. The parents of these eggs were caught off-guard by two thieving monitor lizards working together.

Saltwater crocodile hatchlings

Hatching

Hatchlings squeak to let their mother know they are ready to come out of their egg. High-pitched squeaks from inside the shells bring the mother to scrape off the nest covering that kept them warm.

A mother crocodile makes a nest on land where her eggs can be kept safe and warm. She makes it in the same place every year. She lays the eggs at night, a few at a time, and covers them over.

SEARCH & FIND & SEARCH & FIND

Can you find the kingfisher?

Caring for young

A mother crocodile has a pouch in the bottom of her mouth. As soon as her babies hatch, she picks them up and carries them in her pouch, taking them carefully to the water.

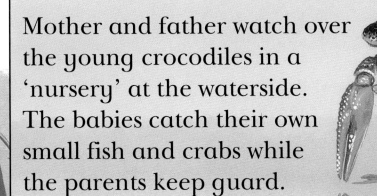

Mother and father watch over the young crocodiles in a 'nursery' at the waterside. The babies catch their own small fish and crabs while the parents keep guard.

Mugger crocodile

Crocodile and alligator babies cannot look after themselves very well. A young alligator may hitch a ride on its mother's back.

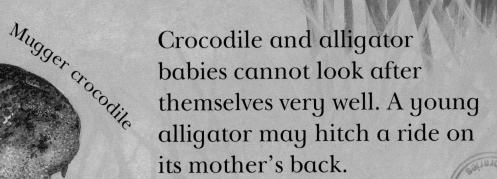

Stockton Borough Public Libraries

Biggest and smallest

Some crocodiles swim in the sea. The estuarine – or saltwater – crocodile from south-east Asia and Australia is the biggest of all crocodiles. It is also the only one to swim in the sea, it lives in *estuaries* along the coast.

SEARCH & FIND Can you find five turtles? FIND SEARCH &

Australian aboriginal art often contains pictures of crocodiles. This is because according to their ancient beliefs the spirits of the dead live on in crocodiles.

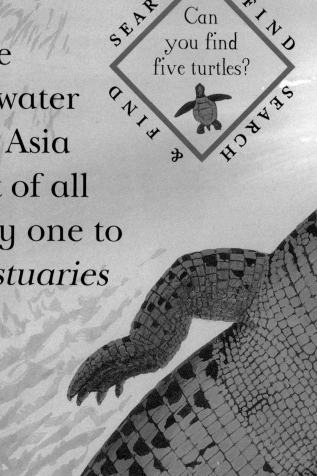

Saltwater crocodile

True or false?

Crocodiles always eat meat.

Answer: **False**

The rare African dwarf crocodile lives in swamps and slow rivers. It eats fish and frogs and also fruit!

The ancient Egyptian god of water, Sobek, was in the shape of a crocodile. This is how he looked in paintings. Use modelling clay to make your own pendant. Don't forget to make a hole for the chain, shoelace, string or ribbon.

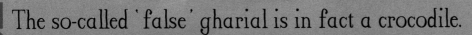

The so-called 'false' gharial is in fact a crocodile.

Hibernation

Alligators dig holes and passages underground where they escape heat and cold. Chinese alligators and the most northernly American alligators sleep through winter, *hibernating* in these tunnels.

SEARCH & FIND
Can you find the snake?
FIND & SEARCH

There are only 600 of these Chinese alligators left living in the wild. They are protected by law but *poachers* still kill them for their skins and meat.

The dwarf caiman from the Amazon basin is one of the smallest alligators. Caimans live in South America. They have armour on their backs and their bellies.

There have been reports of alligators using sewers as their tunnels.

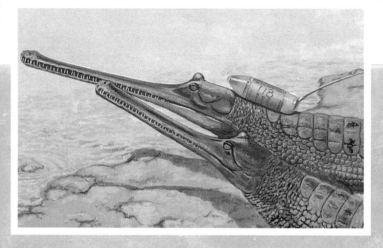

In 1972 crocodile hunting was banned in Australia. It is thought that around 270,000 saltwater crocodile skins and between 200,000 and 300,000 freshwater crocodile skins were exported from Australia before the ban.

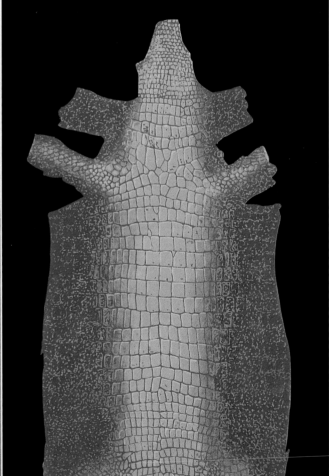

Scientists can learn about crocodiles by fitting them with radio transmitters. That way they can keep track of the crocodiles' movements and find out where they go.

Crocodiles and humans

Some crocodiles and alligators live on farms. They are reared by farmers and sold for their meat and their skins. Farming makes poaching less likely. The farms have also become tourist attractions.

Some people like to keep baby broad-nosed caimans as pets. They look cute when they are very small, but are less fun when they grow bigger!

Glossary

Cold-blooded

Animals that take their heat from the temperature outside are cold-blooded.

Crocodilian

The ancient reptile family which includes crocodiles, alligators, caimans and gharials.

Digest

What an animal's body does with food before taking the nutrients into the bloodstream.

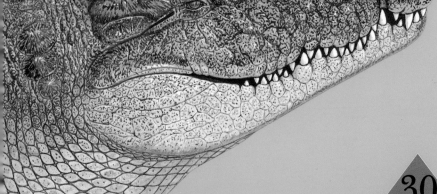

Display

The way in which animals show off to each other, for example, when a peacock spreads its tail feathers.

Estuary

The place where a river runs into the sea.

Fossils

Remains of plants and animals in the rocks. These remains can be dated to show how many millions of years ago a particular plant or animal lived.

Freshwater

Freshwater creatures are

found inland in rivers, streams and lakes – not in the salt water of the sea.

Hatchling
An animal that has just come out of its egg.

Hibernate
To sleep through the winter.

Parasite
A creature that lives off other creatures, for example a flea.

Poachers
Hunters who hunt animals illegally.

Prehistoric
The time long ago

before there were any written records.

Reptile
The animal family to which snakes and crocodiles and dinosaurs all belong.

Territory
An area where an animal lives, which it will defend against outsiders.

Index

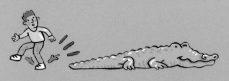

Stockton Borough Public Libraries